SPORTS ENCYCLOPEDIA

RACQUET SPORTS AND ATHLETICS

Om KIDZ
An imprint of Om Books International

Contents

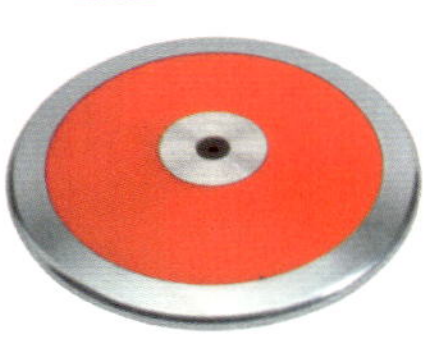

Tennis	4
Table Tennis	6
Badminton	8
Racquetball	9
Basque Pelota	10
Racquets	11
Squash	12
Pickleball	14
Sprint	16
Middle Distance Running	17
Long Distance Running	18
Cross Country Running	19
Hurdles	20
Relay	21
Long Jump	22
Pole Vault	24
Triple Jump	26
Discus Throw	27
Javelin Throw	28
Shot Put	30
High Jump	32

RACQUET SPORTS

Wham! Swish! Crowds cheering with excitement! There are volleys, there are smashes and there are rallies. In most racquet sports, the objective is to hit a ball or a shuttlecock to the opponent in such a way that they are not able to hit back.

Tennis, table tennis, badminton and squash are some of the most popular sports in this category. They are played by people from all over the world. These games are highly competitive in nature. There are thousands of professional sportspersons who are associated with racquet sports. There are also some obscure racquet sports like speedball and qianball which are practised by non-professionals around the world for exercise and recreation.

Racquet sports make for excellent spectator sports. Almost all the games under the umbrella of "racquet sports" require skill, precision and quick thinking along with great stamina and willpower.

Let's take a look at the popular and not-so-popular racquet sports played around the world!

Did you know? Wimbledon is the only tennis championship which takes place on a grass court. The first day of this competition is held on a Monday. It falls between June 20th and 26th every year.

Tennis

Tennis is one of the most popular racquet sports of all time. It is followed by millions of people around the world. It is played as a singles or doubles competition. The equipment needed for tennis is easily available and portable, so it is played by many for recreation.

Origin

Tennis is said to have originated in the northern part of France in the twelfth century. It was invented when a man struck a passing ball with the palm of his hand. Soon it became a sport called "jeu de paume", which was even played by the Louis X of France. It slowly evolved into tennis and grew in popularity with the invention of indoor tennis courts.

The indoor courts were created when Louis X of France expressed his unhappiness in playing the sport outdoors in the thirteenth century. Tennis courts and tennis then spread to all parts of Europe. In the sixteenth century, people began to use tennis racquets instead of their hands. The game got the name "tennis" from the French word "tenez" which means "hold", "receive" or "take".

The popularity of tennis dropped in the eighteenth and nineteenth centuries. Much later, once the modern lawn mowers were invented and indoor yards were properly maintained, the popularity of the game rose again.

Equipment

To play tennis, you need a racquet and a tennis ball. The International Tennis Federation (ITF) has certain rules that need to be followed for the manufacture of the tennis racquets:

1. The hitting area, consisting of woven strings, must be flat and uniform. The frame may not be more than 29 inches in length and 12.5 inches in width.

2. The racquet must have a uniform shape, size and weight distribution. It shouldn't provide any kind of communication to the player during a match.

The weight, size and shape of the tennis racquet has been fixed by the ITF. The hitting area has strings which are of uniform length and distance.

The ball is made of hollow rubber with a felt coating. Though tennis balls were originally white, different colours are used now, with yellow being the preferred colour.

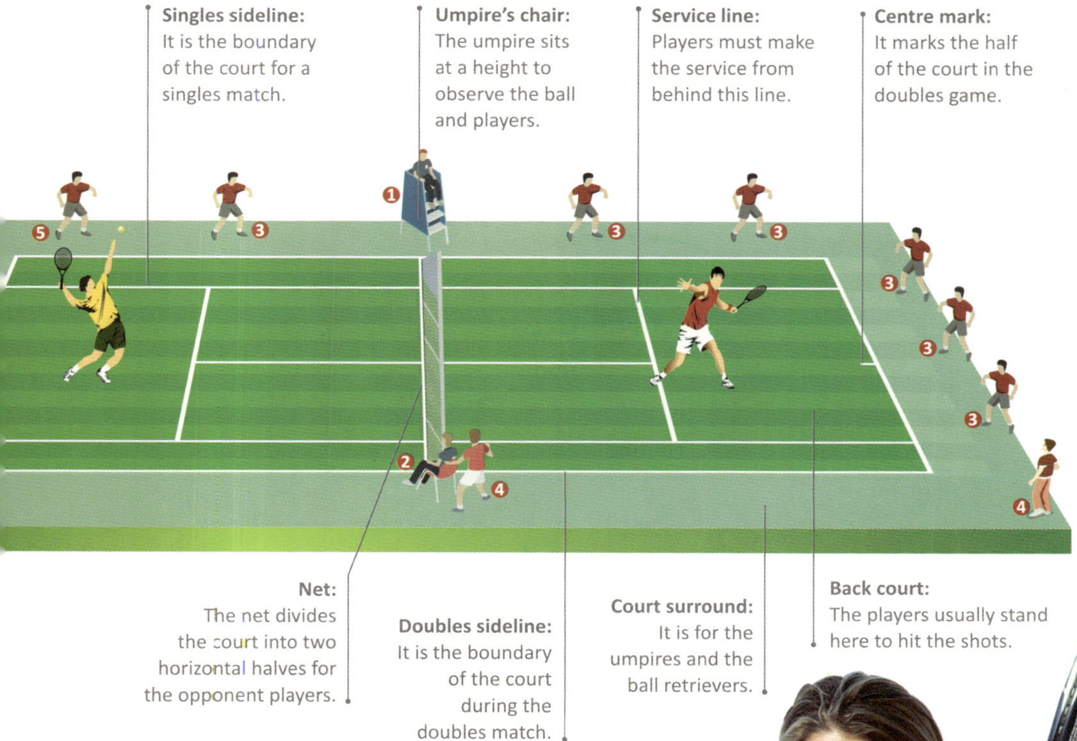

There are four main types of shots that all tennis players need to know:

1. **Serve:** The serve or service shot starts a point or rally. The ball is thrown into the air and hit with the racquet to send it to the opponent's team.
2. **Forehand:** A forehand shot starts at the right side of the body, continues across and ends at the left side after contact is made with the ball.
3. **Backhand:** The backhand shot is for right-handed players and follows the opposite format of the forehand shot.
4. **Volley:** When a player hits the tennis ball from the opponent before it bounces in his court, it is called a volley shot.

Besides the above mentioned shots, there is also the half volley shot where players return the ball to the opponent after it has made just one bounce in their side of the court.

The lob shot sends the ball over the opponent's head and to the back court, making them run far and fast to hit the shot. If the opponent is far away from the net, then a drop shot is used to spike the ball close to the net so that the opponent misses the shot.

Wall of fame

Swiss tennis player Roger Federer has a record 19 Grand Slam singles titles. He is one of the most dominant and greatest men's players of all time.

Spanish left-handed tennis player Rafael Nadal Parera is the finest clay-court player in the history of tennis. He has won 15 Grand Slam single titles.

Ranked first by the Women's Tennis Association, German player Stefanie "Steffi" Graf has won 22 Grand Slam singles titles.

Fact card

- The French Open, known as the Roland Garros, is named after a French pilot from World War I.
- John McEnroe, Martina Navratilova, Serena Williams and Kim Clijsters have won major tournaments without losing a single set over the entire year. John McEnroe did this thrice.
- Martina Navratilova and Pam Shriver have won 21 grand-slam doubles titles.

Table Tennis

Table tennis (TT) is also called ping pong. It is like a miniature tennis game. It is played indoors on a flat table with markings on it. The racquets and ball used are much smaller in size.

The ball weighs exactly 2.7 g. Its diameter is 40 mm. The ball is made of celluloid and filled with air.

The racquet is made of laminated wood which is covered with a rubber sheet. Many players use different rubbers on different sides of the racquet to achieve the spinning and slowing of the ball.

Origin

Table tennis originated in the nineteenth century. Although the root of it is unknown, it is believed that sport was invented by the British officers serving in countries overseas. After dinner, they would set up a barrier of books at the centre of a table, and two books were used to shuttle a golf ball back and forth across this barrier. During the early days, people used all sorts of makeshift equipment like box lids and pieces of corks to play. With its increasing popularity, manufacturers eventually began to create equipments exclusively for table tennis.

James Gibb notably brought about the concept of table tennis as it is played today. When he found out that the celluloid balls were being sold as a novelty item in the USA, he realised that those balls were ideally suited to play the game. While the paddles or the racquets were developed independently by the contribution of various people, James Gibbs single handedly developed the tennis ball.

Earlier, racquets were made of pieces of parchment stretched upon a wooden frame. The sound the frame made when it hit against the ball was similar to the word "ping pong", so this is where the sport got its other name.

Played all over the world today, table tennis is internationally governed by the International Table Tennis Federation (ITTF) which was created in 1926.

The game was included in the Olympics since 1988. Due to the rapid pace of the game, table tennis has become a fun spectator sport all around the world.

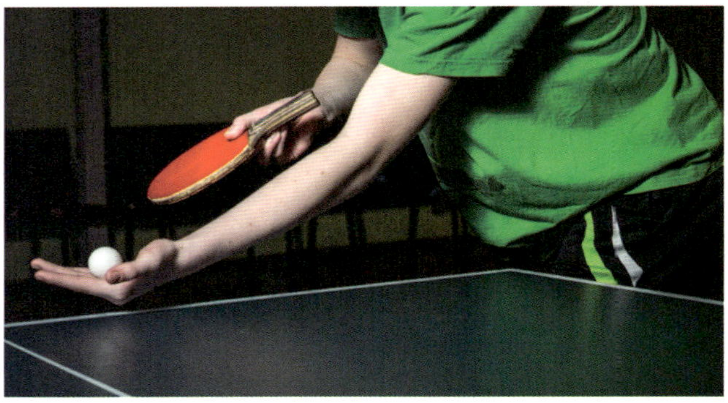

Specifications

Table tennis is played on a 9×5 foot table. The table is usually two and a half feet height. The surface is painted over to resemble the tennis court. The surface needs to give a uniform and sufficient bounce to the ball.

The two sides of the racquet must be painted red and black respectively. This helps a player understand through which side his/her opponent is hitting the ball regardless of the speed.

A table tennis match starts with a coin toss to decide which player will make the first serve. The players must attempt to bounce the ball once on the opponent's side of the net. The player who gets 11 points first, wins the game.

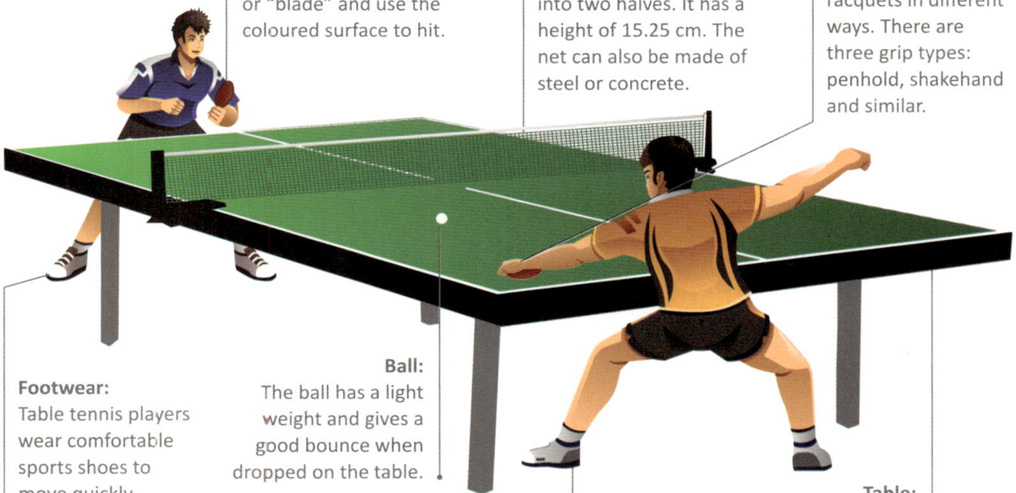

The player is using the forehand move to hit the ball. If the black side of the racquet is visible to the opponent, it means the player is using the backhand.

Adding a spin to the ball drastically changes the gameplay experience. Players need to understand how every offensive hit, defensive hit and serve cause the spin effect on the ball. The backspin, topspin, sidespin and corkspin are the four main types of spin moves.

Wall of fame

Jan Ove Waldner, a Swedish TT player, has won one Olympic gold, two World Championships and one World Cup for the singles round for men. He is one of the most popular TT players today.

Deng Yaping from China has won four Olympic championships, six World Championships and one World Cup for singles round for women.

Liu Guoliang from China has won one Olympic medal, one World Championship and one World Cup for singles round for men.

Fact card

- Hit, loop, counter-hit, flick and smash are the names given to the offensive hits available in TT.
- Push, chop, block and lob are the names of the defensive hits available in the sport of TT.
- The Republic of China has dominated the sport of TT to such an extent that the other countries that play TT are left fighting for the second place.

Badminton

The shuttlecock has a cork base which has feathers attached to it. This is why the shuttlecock is light.

Badminton is a racquet sport in which the players on the field hit a feathered shuttlecock instead of a ball. It is similar to tennis in some ways.

Origin

British officers living in India invented a game in the 1800s to pass time and get exercise. It was called "the game of battledore and shuttlecock". Initially, the game was played with a piece of cork with feathers stuck on it. It was sent back and forth between the players. Back then, the game was also known as "poona" after the town where it was played. The modern name of "badminton" comes from the name of the estate of the Dukes of Beaufort in Gloucestershire. It was there that the modern version of the game was first played in 1873. The Badminton World Federation has been regulating the sport on an international level since its formation in 1934.

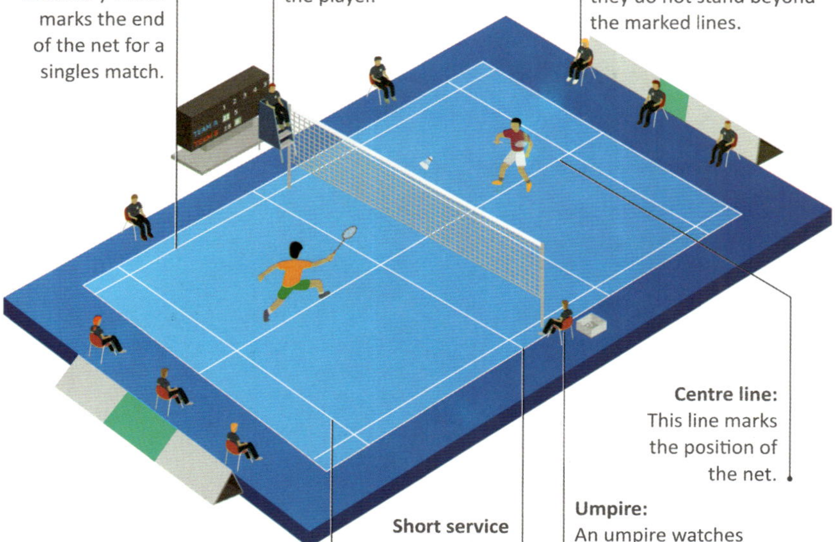

Specifications

On an amateur level, badminton is played in an outdoor field or open area. However, on a professional level, it is played indoors as even the lightest breeze can affect the course of the shuttlecock.

Indoor badminton courts are rectangular and have a measure of 44 feet by 20 feet. Only 17 feet of the width of the court is available for the singles matches. The court has a net strung at a height of five feet to separate the two sides.

The frame of a badminton racquet is made of materials like carbon, fibre, aluminium or even steel. The strings are made of high-quality polymer. As a result, the racquets are light but good for sending the shuttlecock on its way.

Fact card

- Badminton is claimed to be the fastest racquet sport. The fastest shot was a smash hit by Tan Boon Hoeng. The shuttlecock travelled at a speed of 493 kmph during the shot.

Racquetball

Racquetball is an indoor sport which does away with the net used in most racquet sports. Here, the players make use of the walls, floor and ceiling of the playing area to bounce the ball.

Origin

The sport was originally played as "paddleball". In 1950, Joseph Sobek created "racquetball" by replacing paddle sticks with a racquet. In 1976, Ian Wright then Americanised the sport by changing some details like the court in which it is played and the ball which is used.

These players are playing in an outdoor racquetball court. Notice that the player in white is wearing an eyeguard.

Court

The most important part of a racquetball court is the front wall. It is a rectangular court. The front wall is at a height of 20 feet. The court is 40 × 20 feet in dimensions. The service and reception areas are usually marked with broad red lines.

Equipment

The players need a racquetball, which is usually made of rubber and has a 57 mm diameter. They also need racquets, which are specially designed for the game. These racquets have a length of 22 inches. During professional competitions, players wear racquetball eye guards to protect the eyes from the fast-moving ball.

This is an indoor racquetball court. As both players play on the same side, the court is much smaller than a tennis or badminton court.

Rules

The server starts the game by bouncing the ball on the floor once, and then directly hitting the ball on the front wall. He is allowed to bounce the ball off a sidewall after hitting the front wall. However, the ball should not be hit more than three times or against the three walls before it touches the floor. This is a foul.

If the opponent misses a shot after the player makes a serve, then the player gets one point and makes another serve. However, if the player misses the shot, then the opponent does not get a point. Instead, the opponent now makes the next serve.

The racquetball racquet looks quite different from the racquets used in other racquet sports.

Fact card

- Racquetball is very similar to the British game of racketball, except that in the latter, the ceiling is out of bounds.

Basque Pelota

Basque pelota is a variety sport where a player can use a racquet, bat, or even his/her own hand to hit the ball against a wall. In the traditional form of the game, two teams play the game by sending the ball over a line on the ground, or over a net.

These players are using the wooden bat made in Argentina.

Origin

Basque pelota has most likely been derived from the game of "jeu de paume" played in France. Since, the Basques in the mountainous regions of the Pyrenees did not have much access to the modern courts and fancy equipment, it did not develop in the route of tennis. The game looks much like jeu de paume even today. However, there have been some changes, such as the introduction of a special basket-shaped racquet called "chistera", which is unique to this game.

Today, the International Federation of Basque pelota regulates the many different forms of the game. There are four main forms and 14 disciplines.

The Basque paleta court is called a "Fronton".

Rules

The game is played between two teams. The serving team bounces the ball on the floor first and then hits the front wall in between the high line and low line marked on it.

After the serve, the players attempt to bounce the ball off various walls and the floor. This is the rallying part of the game.

If the ball touches the floor more than once, it is considered a "dead shot". This awards a point to the opponent team who was not responsible for the ball touching the floor. The ball needs to rebound off the floor and the front wall and go out of the playing area.

Basque pelota is classified into the below seven forms according to the ball being used to play the sport:

1. Hand Pelota (similar to hand ball)
2. Paleta Goma (uses a rubber ball)
3. Paleta Cuero (uses a leather ball)
4. Pala and Pala Corta (uses a long and a short bat)
5. Jai alai and joko garbi (uses the chistera)
6. Remonte
7. Xare

Eyeguards are important for the safety of the players.

This player is using an Argentinian version of the bat. It is made of wood.

Fact card

- Jai alai literally means the "merry festival".
- The skill of hurling a ball from a chistera has also been used in combat by the peasants of the Basque region.

Racquets

Racquets (called "Rackets" in American English) is an indoor racquet sport. It is mainly played in the USA, United Kingdom, Ireland and Canada. It is very similar to squash, so it is also called "hard racquets". This sport was invented in the eighteenth century. It is an ancient sport which was first played by prisoners.

The racquet used in this game is much like the racquet used in squash.

Origin

Racquets was played as a pastime in the Fleet debtors prisons. It is a modification of another old game called "fives", where the ball is hit by tennis racquets instead of the hand. This way, the sport became quicker. The sport was played against the prison wall. The sport then gained popularity in pubs, schools and construction sites.

The first professional match of racquets was recorded back in 1846. It was played in a racquet court built in Eglinton Castle, where the floor was made of granite slabs. In fact, this court is the oldest surviving court in the world.

It gained popularity with the publication of "The Book of Racquets" by J. R. Atkins in 1872. It was then reprinted in 1981 to commemorate the World Racquets Challenge Match between W. J. C. Surtees and J. A. N. Prenn.

Rules

Racquets is played in singles and doubles matches on courts which have smooth stone or concrete floors. Players use wooden racquets called "bats". The ball used is usually white in colour. The players must strike the ball and hit it against the wall. The ball should hit the wall at a height above 67 cm before bouncing off on the floor. It can also bounce against a side wall before touching the floor or the side wall.

The opponents who are answering the strike can hit the ball after it has bounced on the floor once, or even hit a volley shot.

The world championship racquet game is held for singles and doubles, and is made in a challenge format. The challengers play against the reigning champion, who has won the most matches in a 14-game format. This challenger system is slowly changing to a tournament system. Tournaments are hosted in the USA and United Kingdom.

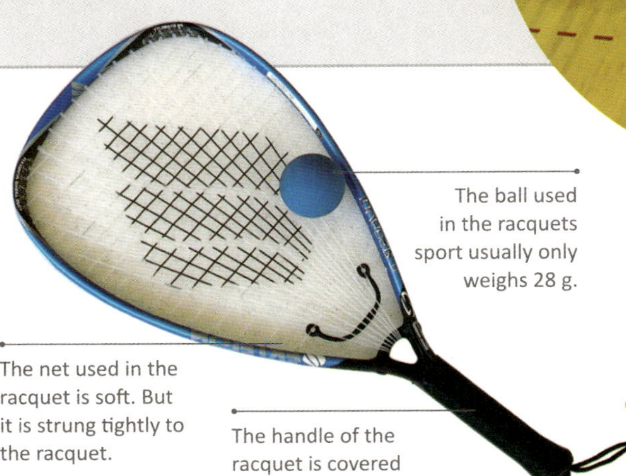

The ball used in the racquets sport usually only weighs 28 g.

The net used in the racquet is soft. But it is strung tightly to the racquet.

The handle of the racquet is covered with soft material for a tight grip.

Fact card

- Charles Dickens referred to this game in his 1836 novel, *The Pickwick Papers*.

Squash

Squash is similar to the game of racquets, where the opponents stand next to each other facing a wall. They bounce the ball off the wall repeatedly in a rallying style, until one of them misses the shot.

Origin

Squash has actually descended from the game of racquets. It was invented by school children who played the game in narrow enclosed spaces. The name is derived from the fact that the rubber ball gets squashed against the wall when it bounces against it.

The game originated in 1830 in Harrows School, England. It was played with shortened tennis racquets by the children from that school. It soon became popular in other boarding schools as well. However, it was only after World War I that squash as a game really caught on in the public imagination. Club courts had already appeared in various parts of Britain by the 1900s. As the game overtook racquets in terms of popularity, rules began to be formalised and the Squash Rackets Association was formed to regulate it.

In the USA, a slightly smaller court was used along with a lawn tennis ball and a lawn tennis racquet. This version was called "squash tennis", and the normal squash was referred to as "squash racquets". Slowly, squash racquets overtook squash tennis in terms of popularity until the game was almost completely supplanted. However, even today, the USA uses a different ball to play squash. Hardball squash is another, tougher variation of this sport. Today, squash is recognised by the IOC. In fact, proponents of the game are lobbying to have it included in the Olympics in the near future.

The two women in this picture are playing a squash doubles match. They are also wearing comfortable cotton clothes which fir their form tightly.

The player is attempting to hit a ball that has just bounced from the floor. Hence, the squash racquet is held at a low angle. She is hoping to raise the ball up to a height.

The ball is soft and small. Hit with lots of force, this ball bounces back from the wall with great speed.

The squash racquet is larger than the racquetball racquet.

The strings are equidistant and laid parallel to each other, and are wound tightly into the frame.

The positioning of the leg is also important. But trained players move their legs subconsciously.

Rules

The rules of squash are slightly difficult to visualise, though the game is fairly easy to play. The international squash courts are 32 feet long and 21 feet wide. The front wall has a "service line", above which the player must hit the ball. This line extends all the way over the sidewalls and continues onto the back wall.

Basically there is an area demarcated by lines and the ball must bounce within that area.

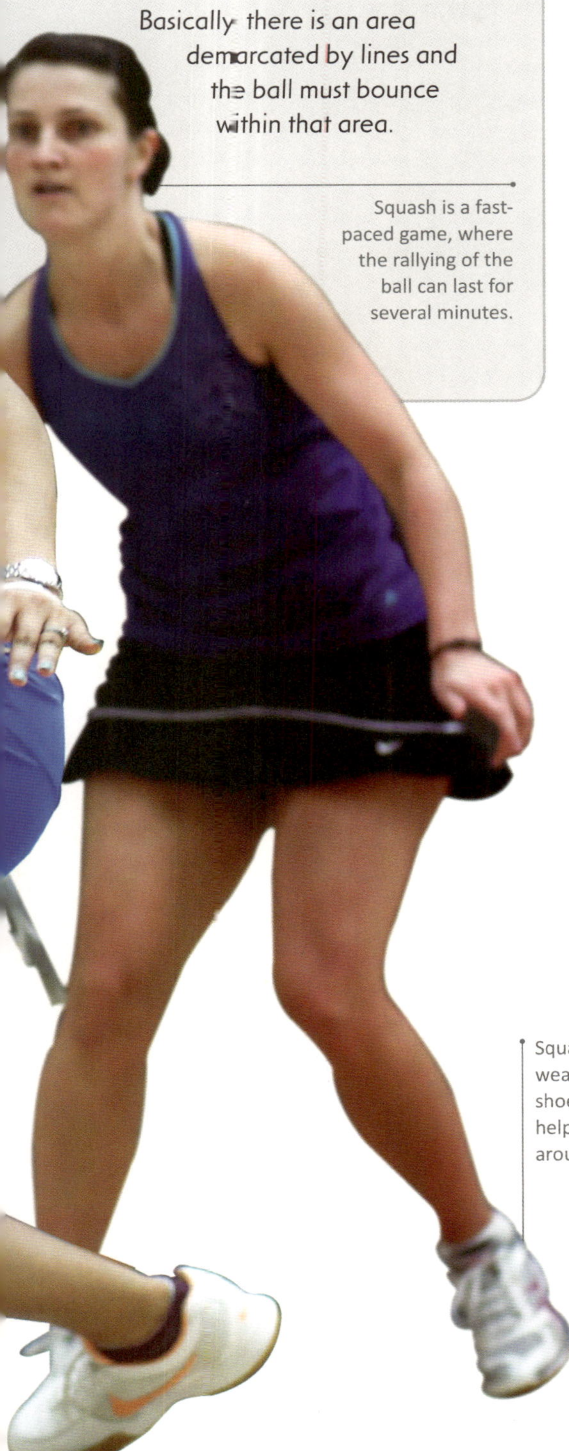

Squash is a fast-paced game, where the rallying of the ball can last for several minutes.

This picture shows a player hitting back the ball before it touches the ground.

The court is divided into three parts: the front half, the left back quarter and the right back quarter.

The player must stand in one quarter and bounce the ball off the front wall in such a way that it lands in the other quarter, before the opponent can hit it. That is a valid of way of serving. After serving, a player again bounces the ball in such a manner that the opponent fails to return it.

In the British way of playing squash, only the server may score. If he/she fails, the serve is passed onto the opponent. In the USA however, either player may score. International matches followed the British method for a while before recently adapting the American system.

Squash racquets are light and the strings are made of high quality polymers. The ball is a synthetic soft construct.

Some of the most important shots of the squash game are straight dive (to hit the ball parallel to the side wall) and boast (to hit the ball off a side wall at a strategic angle before it hits the front or back wall).

Squash players wear sports shoes which help them move around easily.

The two yellow dots on the ball indicate that experienced players use this ball as it gives a low bounce.

Wall of fame

The greatest squash player, Jahangir Khan from Pakistan, became the Youngest World Amateur Champion in 1979.

Malaysian squash player Nicol David is the first Asian woman to get the first place rank in squash. She became world number 1 in January 2006.

Ramy Ashour is amongst the top ten squash players of all time. At the age of 22, he was one of the youngest players to become world number 1.

In women's squash, Michelle Martin, Heather McKay and Sarah Fitz-Gerald from Australia deserve a special mention.

Fact card

- Forbes magazine declared squash as the perfect sport to maintain fitness and health.
- Protective eyegear like thick goggles are used for safety reasons in this game as the ball can bounce around with great speed inside the court.

Pickleball

Certain sports evolve less out of a specific goal and more out of unusual circumstances. Pickleball is one such sport that combines aspects of multiple games, like tennis, badminton and table tennis.

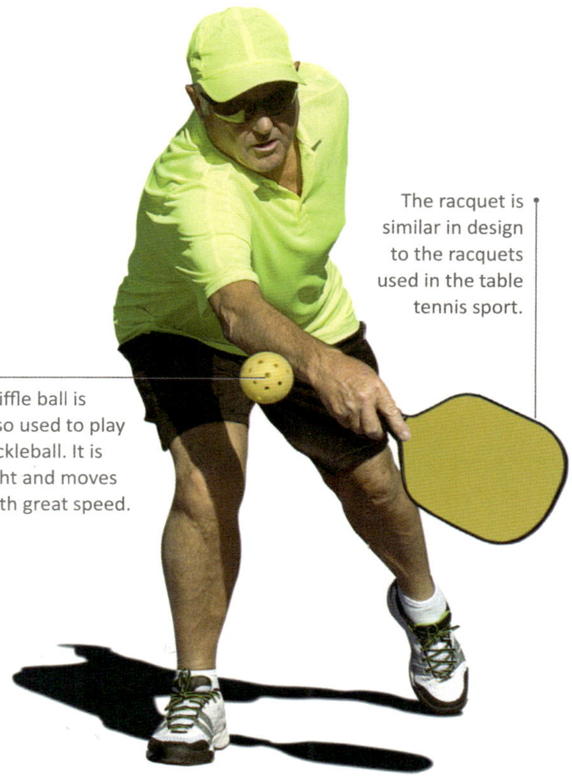

The racquet is similar in design to the racquets used in the table tennis sport.

Wiffle ball is also used to play pickleball. It is light and moves with great speed.

Origin

Pickleball is a hybrid sport. Joel Pritchard invented the game in 1965 at Bainbridge, Washington, USA.

One afternoon, when Joel returned from playing golf with his friends, they found that their families were bored, with nothing to do on a Saturday. Hence, they decided to play badminton, but they didn't have either the ball or a racquet, or a court. So, they took a wiffle ball and raised the net on the tennis court in the house.

The racquets were carved out of some leftover wood. It is because of this that the game got the name of "pickleball". As Joel had mentioned, "it reminded me of the Pickle Boat in crew, where oarsmen were chosen from the leftovers of other boats".

Rules

The game starts with a service shot. The serve is made with an underhand stroke. The player hits the ball from below the waist or navel level. The ball is hit in such a way that it has an upward arc from the baseline, which is diagonal to the opponent's service zone. Points only go to the serving side. Usually, points are scored when the opponents miss a shot or one of their shots turns out to be foul. If the service team misses a shot, the opponent gets a chance to serve.

In the doubles game, the serving side is allowed one fault serve. If they make another, they lose their chance to serve. Then the opponent's take up the serve. After the first service shot, each side gets to make two faults before the serve is transferred to the other team. So, in this game, the score usually ends with one serve ahead, behind or in a tie.

Even players in wheelchairs can play this game. For those in wheelchairs, very minor changes have been made to the rules. Wheelchairs are considered a part of the player's body.

A player should not touch the baseline, sideline or centre line around the player. A return service cannot be volleyed. It needs to bounce by the server.

A pickleball match in progress.

Fact card

- Many people think that pickleball was named after Joel's dog, Pickles. But actually, the dog was named after the game.
- Joel Pritchard went on to become the State Representative of Washington in the 1970s.
- There are mixed games where standing players and wheelchair players play together.

ATHLETICS

The term "athletic" is often used as an adjective to describe a young, vigorous and healthy person. Athletics refer to a group of sports that require almost no equipment but are designed to test the athlete's physical fitness.

Athletics have their origins in the martial training that was imparted to the recruits. All recruits were supposed to be able to run a certain distance and jump certain obstacles.

This training session slowly evolved into a competition, where everyone aimed to be the fastest in covering a certain distance or to jump the farthest. This particular format has been popular in Athletics for thousands of years now. The ancient Greek writings mention Athletics and the various athletes extensively. The Ancient Olympics happened to be a large event and possibly the greatest gathering of athletes in the ancient world.

Did you know? It has been established that the average world class athlete trains approximately 23 hours a week. Interestingly, the average athlete in America trains approximately 12 hours a week.

Sprint

Men have been dashing about since the ancient times. Prehistoric men ran to catch their prey and to avoid being preyed upon. Speed always had an immense value in survival. As a result, sprint, or running as a sport, is ancient.

Origin

Sprint was one of the sports played at the Ancient Olympics. The sole aim of this game is to compete to be the fastest among others, in reaching the end of the arena. This distance was known as one "stadion" in Greek. A "stadion" could vary in length based on the location. Its length ranged from 177–192 m..

The sport is very common; it requires nothing more than some open space. Sprinting has been a part of several other sports as well. In sprint, the players don't cover a distance more than 400–440 m.

Beyond a certain distance limit, human beings are unable to maintain the high speed, due to the formation of lactic acid in muscles. A distance as short as 60 m is insufficient, to provide proper acceleration to the players.

Spikes at the bottom of the shoes to maintain a grip on the ground.

Lightweight shoes worn by runners to maintain speed.

A starting block used by runners to brace their feet.

Rules

All the players start off together, either by standing in a line or by being staggered around a curve. At the referee's signal, they dash off simultaneously.

Earlier, the runners had to take a standing start. However, since 1884, runners use a block to brace their feet. This is known as a "starting block".

A race being run amongst the sprinters running in their own lanes.

A stopwatch used to time the sprinters.

Fact card

- Jamaican sprinter Usain Bolt is popularly nicknamed "Lightning Bolt".

The interesting part is that even the smallest race run in someone's school or amongst friends starts the same way as the formal ones. The only difference is probably the gun shot at the end.

The referee usually starts off by uttering the following: "Everybody on your marks. Get set. Go!" He then fires the gun. This is the cue that the sprinter has to start sprinting now. Anybody who starts running before the gunshot is considered to have made a false start. This could end up in the sprinter being disqualified or seconds being added to his final time.

Since sprints mostly take place on a curved track, the lanes are drawn on them. This is to ensure that all sprinters cover the same distance. Sprinters must stay in their respective lanes. If a sprinter leaves his lane, knowingly or unknowingly, it could result in disqualification or again, seconds being added to the final time of the sprinter.

Middle Distance Running

It is physically impossible for a player to sustain a sprint for more than 35 seconds. Beyond that, one's stamina and endurance go for a toss. A sport in which the players cover a distance longer than a sprint, but short enough to cover a flat-out run, is the "middle distance".

Tight clothes are worn to make the body more aerodynamic.

Swinging the hands enables the runner to have better control over the heart rate.

Light comfortable shoes are worn to help with speed.

Origin

A mile was generally considered as an adequate distance, which required both speed and stamina. As a result, running a mile was a test of skill and raw talent. The shortest middle distance running is usually of 600 m whereas the longest ones are around 3000 m. Originally, 880 m or half a mile was a common middle distance range until it was replaced by the 800 m race. This was largely because of the adoption of the metric system over the imperial system.

A middle distance running race in progress.

Rules

The rules for middle distance running are similar to those of sprint. Runners have to wait for the starter's gun firing before running. They are set into their respective lanes, and must ensure not to stray into the neighbouring ones. A player going into an inner lane covers a shorter distance than what is prescribed and hence is penalised for the same. The game is measured upon the laps of the track.

The various races covered are:

- 600 m (obsolete)
- 800 m
- 880 m (half mile)
- 1500 m
- 1600 m (full mile)
- 2000 m
- 3000 m

Two middle distance running competitors are racing on their lanes in the track.

Fact card

- Middle distance running is different from the sport of sprint as it requires the player to maintain a constant pace and put on a burst of speed at the end.
- The longer end of the spectrum is the 3000 m race. This race is usually a steeplechase for men and a regular run for women.

Long Distance Running

Pheidippides was a Greek soldier and a messenger at the battle of Marathon. Myth has it that he ran from Marathon to Athens to give a message and lost his life doing it. And thus the legendary sport of Marathon, a form of long distance running, was born. Pheidippides was possibly the most famous long distance runner in history.

Origin

Long distance running has been around since the dawn of civilisation. Running long distances was critical when there were no other means of transport. It also helped in building up stamina and endurance. Prehistoric man had to be an excellent runner to hunt down prey. Human beings have evolved optimally to run long distances.

In the modern era, the most common competitive races are held on tracks. The oval track is characteristic of these races, with the runners completing a number of predefined laps. Long distance running has been a part of the Stockholm Olympics since 1912. Women's long distance running was incorporated in 1984.

Marathon runners wear a patch of cloth with their number on it.

Light clothes are worn to allow the skin to breathe as the marathon is a long haul.

Light and comfortable shoes are worn to help them run faster.

Rules

The competitors must start at the starter's gun firing signal and complete a number of predefined laps. The first one to complete all the laps and to reach the finishing line is declared the winner. Players are not allowed to cross their assigned lanes.

Like middle distance running, the runners in this game maintain a strategic pace to sustain their stamina and endurance till the end. Unlike middle distance, there is seldom a final burst of speed.

Longer races, like the Marathons and Ultra Marathons, take place on roads instead of a track.

In a Marathon, the runners jog together as they have to reserve their energy for a long run.

Fact card

- A Marathon race is exactly of 42.195 km, which actually is the distance from Marathon to Athens.
- Ultra Marathons can be over 100 km long!

Cross Country Running

The concept of cross country running is the closest to what prehistoric men actually did to hunt down prey. Let's take a look at it.

Origin

As the name suggests, cross country running is running over natural terrain, including flatlands and hills. Though the sport has been around since ancient times, the first instance of the sport was in the nineteenth century.

In England, people played a game called "Hounds and Hares". One group was the hares and the other was the hounds. The hares would take off and leave scraps of paper as a trail while the hounds gave a chase. The sport started becoming popular when English country clubs started having these runs on their grounds. A famous one was the Crick Run at the Rugby School in 1837.

A cross country running race in progress. Runners wear numbers on their chest that makes it easier to distinguish them.

Communities often organise cross country running to encourage a group spirit amongst neighbours.

Rules

There is no standard distance or terrain for cross country running. However, the International Association of Athletic Federations state that tracks for men must be at least 12 km long, and those for women must be at least 8 km long.

Due to the varying difficulties of the courses, no world records are maintained. Races are judged relatively, i.e., winners are chosen on the basis of the time they take as compared to others. In case of a team event, scores are assigned as one to the first, two to the second and so on. The team with the lowest total wins.

While tracks are not strictly regulated, there are certain guidelines that need to be followed. The track must be clear, with loops and gentle turns. The path must be at least 5 m wide and clearly marked.

Teams of runners run cross country across flatlands and natural courses, encouraging each other to keep up.

Fact card

- Cross Country runners were often called "harriers" after a breed of coursing hounds.

Hurdles

Trying to overcome problems and difficulties is called crossing the "hurdles". There's an athletic event, which is literally based on that concept. Interestingly, the sport is called "hurdles" or "hurdle race".

Runners wear protective goggles to keep their eyes safe from the harsh Sun.

The back leg is almost at a right angle as compared to the rest of the body.

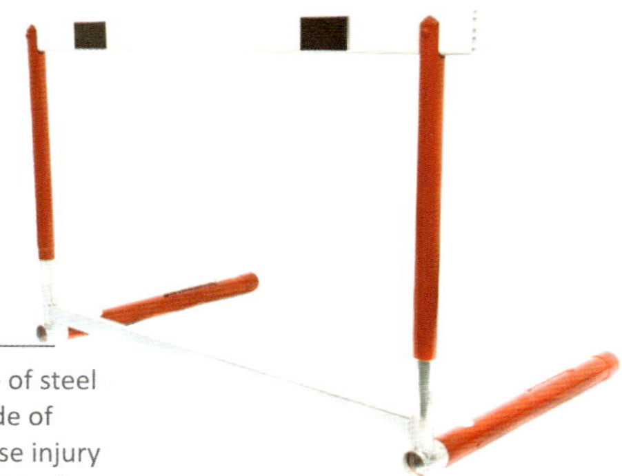

A hurdle is made of steel with the bar made of plastic to minimise injury if someone runs into it.

Origin

The earliest known records of hurdles were at Eton College, around 1837. Hurdling then was a stop-and-go sport. Hurdlers ran towards each hurdle, crossed it and landed on both feet to stop their forward momentum. The hurdles were of different heights. The distance between the hurdles also varied and depended on the height of the hurdles.

A.C.M. Croome from Oxford is considered to be the father of modern hurdles to some extent. He jumped the hurdles with his trunk leaning forward and his back leg almost at a right angle to the rest of his body. This is the basis of the modern technique of hurdles.

A women's hurdle race in progress.

Rules

Hurdlers start on a straight track with the hurdles placed at pre-defined intervals. They must clear the hurdles without touching them or knocking them over. The first person to finish the line by crossing all the hurdles in the correct manner, is declared the winner.

According to the Olympics rules, hurdle races are carried out for distances of 110, 200 and 400 m for men whereas women's hurdle races are restricted to the distances of 100 and 200 m.

The highest hurdles are used for the races run by men. They have a height of 106.7 cm. These are called "college high" or "open high". They are also used for sprint hurdle races.

The "high school high" hurdles are used for men under the age of 50. They have a height of 99.1 cm. They are the second highest hurdles used in races. The intermediate hurdles are used for men's long hurdle races. They have a height of 91.44 cm. The women's short hurdle races use hurdles at the height of 83.8 cm. The "low hurdle" has a height of 76.2 cm and is used for women's long hurdle races.

The hurdles are set as follows:

110 m	10 high hurdles	1.067 m high, placed 9.14 m apart
200 m	10 low hurdles	76.2 cm high, placed 18.29 m apart
400 m	10 intermediate hurdles	91.4 cm high, placed 35 m apart
100 m	10 hurdles	84 cm high

Fact card

- The women's hurdles race was originally contested over 80 m instead of 100 m.
- The hurdles were modified in shape to make it safer for the athletes who accidentally crashed into them.

Relay

There is no "I" in team but there are two in "winning". Relay races work on the same principle, where teams of runners compete on a track. The team completing the race in the lowest overall time is declared the winner.

A relay runner passing the baton to his teammate.

Origin

The first known instance of a relay race happened in the USA around 1883. Relay involves a team of four runners, each of whom run an equal distance.

In the earlier days, the players would run the race by holding flags and would hand over the flag to the next teammate. However, the concept of carrying a flag while running was too cumbersome. Thus, the method was replaced by "touching" the next teammate. One player would touch the next one, enabling him/her to take off.

By 1893, this tradition was also replaced with batons. The baton is a small cylinder of wood or plastic and is handed over to the next player. There are two relay races that take place in the Olympics.

A relay runner at the starting point with the baton in their hand that they have to pass on to their teammate.

Rules

Each player must hand off the baton to the next only within a certain zone, which is marked by triangles on the track. Only then can the next runner start running. The process goes on until the baton is given to the last teammate.

The first runner reaches the second one in a few strides. The second runner then runs with his hand behind him and the first player then hands over the baton.

The relays are of two types; four players running 100 m each and four players running 400 m each. There are also longer races that take place in legs.

Fact card

Longer relays may have multiple legs of up to 16 km each. They are often played overnight.

Long Jump

Often the athletes slip and fall as they land after a long jump, which is why they jump in the sandpit to minimise injuries.

There was the game of high jump, and now there is the game of long jump. As the name suggests, in this game, the players attempt to cover the farthest possible distance by jumping. The motto of the game is well explained by what Captain Kirk from Star Trek said, "to boldly go where no man has ever gone before".

Origin

The long jump sport is a fairly old event, being a part of the ancient Olympics of Greece. It was the only jumping event in the pentathlon.

Originally, the sport of long jump was performed by carrying weights in the hands, which were known as the "halteres". A haltere weighed between 2–9 kg. The runner would take a small run up, then jump and land in an area dug specifically for landing. The halteres were swung to create extra momentum, both during the jump and in mid-air.

Music was played to help the athlete get used to the complex rhythm of jumping. A quote by Philostrates mentioned, "The rules regard jumping as the most difficult of the competitions, and they allow the jumper to be given advantages in rhythm by the use of the flute, and in weight by the use of the haltere."

Rules

The player takes a running start of about 40 m, down a synthetic surface. At the end of this the athlete uses a wooden board as a take-off point to jump into a pit filled with sand or fine gravel.

Crossing the foul line results in a disqualified jump. A watching referee and a patch of plasticine record and rule on a foul. The player can start his jump from any point, but the distance is measured only from the foul line.

Athletes swing their arms forward to gain momentum and cover more distance.

Closely fitting clothes are worn so that they don't interfere with the jump.

Comfortable and light shoes are worn to make it easier to jump and yet maintain balance after landing.

The jumps are attempted in the sand pit which break the fall of the athletes and hence help to avoid any major injuries to them.

The long jump has been a part of the modern Olympics since 1896. However, the long jump for women was introduced only in 1948. An event of long jump can be basically diviced into five parts:

1 **Approach run:** The athlete accelerates to the maximum controllable speed before taking off to jump.

2 **Last two strides:** The athlete partially crouches down to lower his centre of gravity. His/her per ultimate stride is longer than the last one. The final stride is short, as the athlete raises his/her centre of gravity, which provides a vertical impulse.

3 **The takeoff:** The athlete attempts to create the most effective take-off possible.

4 **Air action:** This refers to the athlete's actions to combat the forward rotation, experienced by the athlete.

5 **Landing:** The athlete attempts to land as far forward as possible to maximise the counted distance, since the touch nearest to take-off point is counted for distance.

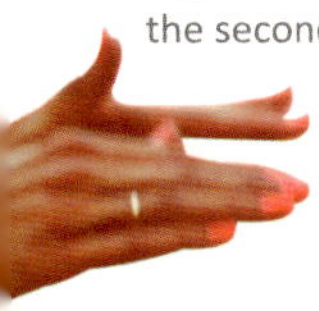

Hitch-kick:
Here, the participant takes off with one leg and the other leg bends behind. Then, the first leg moves forward to land and the second leg follows.

Sail:
Here, the participant takes off and holds that position as long as possible, till he lands at the end.

Hang:
Here, the participant takes off vertically and folds the legs under him while stretching his hands over head.

Wall of fame

Mike Powell from USA has the record of jumping a distance of 8.95 m.

Bob Beamon from USA has the record of jumping a distance of 8.90 m.

Carl Lewis from USA has the record of jumping a distance of 8.87 m.

Galina Chistyakova from USSR has the record of jumping a distance of 7.52 m.

Fact card

- Bob Beamon's record jump was the world record for men's long jump for 23 years, until Mike Powell broke it.
- Three of the longest jumps are by athletes from the USA. Each has broken the previous world record.
- Track and field events are the main motif of collectors' coins. There are Long Jump commemorative coins in the Greek currency.

Pole Vault

So far, we've seen jumpers, who soar with only what nature gave them. However, we always look to get better tools, to go higher and farther. Pole vault developed from such a tradition.

Origin

When the marshes filled the areas of Friesland and Netherlands, the low-lying fens of Cambridgeshire and other areas were artificially drained. These created drains and canals. They were too wide for people to jump and so, they resorted to using poles to jump and cross them.

Even today, parts of Netherland have poles stacked in the house for crossing the streams. Most competitions held in this region also focus on distance more than height. In Friesland they are known as Fierljeppen.

One of the earliest pole vault instances where the height was measured, happened in Britain in 1843. However, regular instances of modern pole vaulting started in 1850 in Germany, due to initiatives taken by Johann Gutsmuths and Friedrich J. Lahn.

Due to the technique involved, modern version of pole vaulting attracts a lot of gymnasts. In fact, multiple record holders in pole vaulting are also gymnasts. Pole vault has been an Olympics event since 1896 for men and since 2000 for women.

Gameplay

For a track and field sport, pole vault requires more expensive equipment than usual, even for the beginners. The arena consists of a long running strip and a horizontal bar. Both the preparations and rules are similar to the high jump. Each player gets three chances to clear a height, failing which results in elimination.

The equipment and the technique used distinguish pole vault from high jump. The vaulter has a pole in hand. The jump is broken into six stages:

1 **Approach:** A player runs through a stretch of 18 to 22 stride length, where he/she tries to maximise the speed. In the beginning, the pole is carried at an angle. Then, it is moved closer to a horizontal position as the landing pit comes nearer.

2 **Plant and take-off:** The athlete plants the pole in a box designated for this and throws himself/herself first upwards and then forwards.

3 **Swing up:** The athlete swings up with a motion of the hips. His/her legs cross over his/her body and above the pole.

4 **Extension:** With his/her hips, the player pushes the pole down to effectively extend himself/herself upside down, from the end of the pole.

5 **Turn:** The athlete rotates his/her body by 180-degree angle to ensure that the bar is crossed without being touched.

6 **Fly-away:** The athlete pushes the pole away to give himself/herself some forward momentum. This is to ensure that neither the player nor the pole touch the bar and dislodge it.

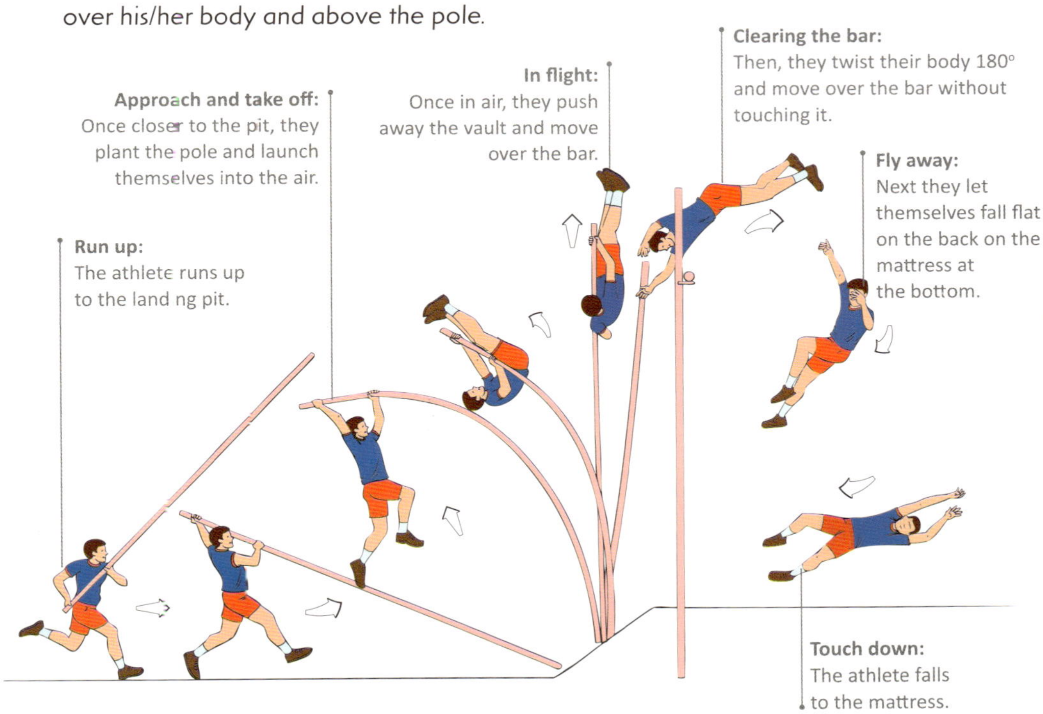

Gymnastics and pole vaulting has a special connection. There are several pole vaulters who have a background in gymnastics. This is because both of these events require the same kind of athletic skills. The running speed of the pole vaulter needs to be fast as well.

Game gear

Sometimes, pole vaulters wear two different types of shoes. On the foot that they use to launch themselves, they wear a shoe with a thick sole, which gives cushioning to the foot. On the other foot, they wear a normal running shoe, or one with spikes to keep their grip on the ground.

Wall of fame

Sergey Bubka from Ukraine has the record of crossing 6.15 m in men's pole vault.

Renaud Lavillenie from France has the record of crossing 6.16 m in men's pole vault.

Yelena Isinbayeva from Russia has the record of crossing 5.06 m in women's pole vault.

Fact card

- The player is allowed to change the distance between the bar and the box where the pole is set in the ground.
- Poles were initially made of solid ash. Today, exotic materials like carbon fibre with a metallic core are used.
- Poles today are pre-bent to ensure that they bend in the right direction.
- Sergey Bubka's long standing record of 6 m was eventually broken by Renaud Lavillenie who jumped 6.16 m.

Triple Jump

The phrase "hop, skip and a jump away", is used to describe something that is a short distance away. But when the term is used for an Olympic athlete, it is associated with a sport called the "triple jump", the distance for which is not so short, either. A triple jump is a long jump, preceded by two short hops.

An athlete attempting the long jump at the end of the triple jump.

Origin

The ancient Olympics have records of people jumping up to 15 m or more! Historians believe that those couldn't have been achieved with one jump but rather by a series of jumps. And this led to the birth of the triple jump.

The triple jump involves an athlete hopping twice and then taking off in a long jump. The triple jump was a part of the inaugural Olympic Games, in 1896. The jumper had to take off from a standstill, hop twice on the same foot and then launch into a long jump.

This is referred to as a "standing triple jump", which is outmoded at the present time. The women's triple jump was introduced in the Atlanta Olympics, in 1996.

A woman athlete landing after a triple jump.

The mud pit in which the triple jump is performed.

Fact card

- In Irish mythology, the "geal-ruith" (triple jump) was an event contested in the ancient Irish Tailteann Games, as far back as 1829 BCE.

Rules

The rules of triple jump, are pretty similar to long jump. The athlete sprints down to the launch board, from where the distance of the jump is measured. The board may have a rectangle painted on it, to show the optimal jumping point. There is also a strip of clay or plasticine at the edge of this point. Touching this is automatically considered to be a "foul".

According to the rules, when the athlete attempts his jump, he has to first land on the same foot as the one he started on. Then he has to hop on the next foot, and the last jump ends with both the feet on the ground.

The game of triple jump occurs in three phases:

1 **Hop:** The athlete takes off from the board on one foot, focusing on the forward momentum. The athlete paws the foot backward for additional momentum, while landing on the other.

2 **Bound:** The athlete takes off immediately, to gain additional momentum through his/her hips.

3 **Jump:** Unlike a long jump, the final jump is performed with much less speed.

Discus Throw

Homer's Odyssey had a description of Odysseus hurling a discus, "farther than the eye could follow". This is one of the oldest surviving accounts of discus throw. Let's take a look at the sport!

Athletes must twist to gather momentum to launch a discus.

They take support from their knee when twisting.

They wear comfortable shoes with a good grip.

Origin

The discus throw has been around since the ancient times. A discus was used in combat, in ancient Greece. Homer mentions the game in both, the Iliad as well as the Odyssey. The fifth century BCE statue in Greece called "discobolus", is further evidence of the game being present during that era.

The very first men's event of discus throw was held at the inaugural edition of the modern Summer Olympics, in 1896. During the 1896 game, participants created fun-raising stamps. During the 1920 and 1948 Summer Olympics, throwers were featured on the main poster. Women were roped into the sport at the Olympics level only in 1928.

Evolution

Discus throw, initially, had an elaborate style, which focused majorly on the hurling. Athletes tried to emulate the paintings and drawings of Ancient Greek athletes. The throw was made from an inclined pedestal.

This became outmoded, when a seven foot circle was introduced. The athletes then had to whirl one and a half times in the circle, before releasing the discus. The circle was further enlarged to its present size of 8.2 feet, in 1912.

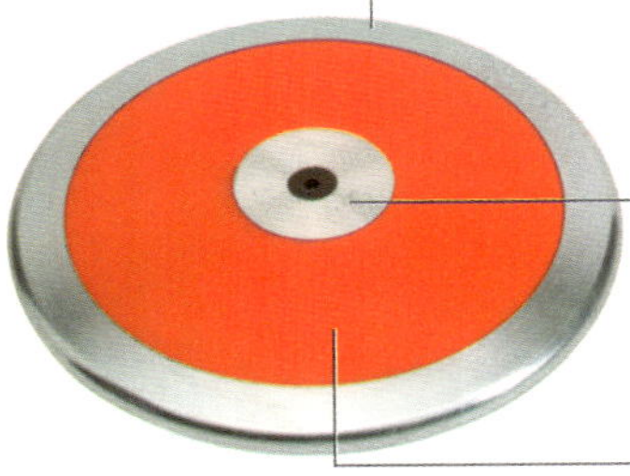

The outer edge of the discuss is metallic. The player grips the discuss around this edge.

The centre of the discus is also made of metal. Originally stone was used, now it is made out of bronze, iron or lead.

The body of the discus is light and made of plastic.

Technically, a discus throw technique can be broken down into five different phases. During a discus throw, the athlete must deliver the discus at top speed. The correct method is to build up the torque so that the maximum force is applied to the discus.

Fact card

- The discus throw was a part of the heptathlon at the ancient Olympics, but not the modern ones.

Javelin Throw

"Ready javelins! Present! Release!" The legionnaires all threw their light spears at the advancing column, making it look like a porcupine. Javelin throw was developed to train legionnaires in the Roman Army.

An athlete attempting the javelin throw.

Origin

The Javelin is a light, throwing spear that is both shorter and lighter than a full spear. Spearmen are exceedingly effective at piercing armour, but they lack range. On the contrary, archers have great range, but cannot pierce heavy shields and armour. The javelin was developed combining the best traits of both.

The major difference between ancient and modern javelins is the weight. Ancient javelins were made heavy to penetrate through thick armour. Modern javelins are made light, to focus more on achieving greater range. Another difference is the ancient practice of using a leather thong, called an "ankyle". It was wound around the middle of the shaft. The athletes held the javelin by the ankle. The thong unwound and gave the javelin a spiraled flight when the javelin was released.

Javelin throw is very popular in the Olympic games and is featured for both, men and women category. Mostly, Nordic nations in Europe, i.e., Norway, Sweden and Finland dominate the sport.

Image of the Roman army training to throw javelins.

During the era between the Mycenaean times and the Roman Empire, use of the javelin as an offensive weapon was common.

Finland won the only two-handed javelin throw competition that happened in 1912, sweeping all the medals. The athletes hurled one javelin from each hand.

Female athlete taking a run before the javelin throw.

They wear comfortable clothing that doesn't interfere with the activity.

The clothes are snuggly fitting to keep the athlete from tripping.

The athlete takes a run before launching the javelin into the air.

Game gear

The javelin used for the event has been re-designed multiple times. The grip of the javelin is made from cord. Both the position of the grip and the centre of gravity for the javelin are heavily regulated. The surface area in front of the centre of gravity is higher than that at the back, which reduces lift and increases the tendency of the javelin to tip forward.

As the athletes have to carry the javelin in one hand and run before throwing it, it becomes important that the javelin doesn't slip and fall. Hence, javelins have a grip.

Athletes may not use an "unorthodox" style in the javelin throw. The javelin must be thrown overhand, passing above the shoulder or upper arm, by holding it at the grip. The athlete may not turn around, so his/her back faces the throw. This is to prevent a spin and hurl of the javelin, similar to that of the discus. Instead, athletes may take up to a short running start from a strip. Also, the athlete may not leave the area until the javelin has landed in the 28.69° sector demarcated for the same.

A javelin throw game has five to six rounds, each allowing an individual competitor to throw once.

The longest legal throw decides the fate of a match. If there is a tie in the result, it is resolved by the second longest throw. If a competition has a large number of athletes, then the rule of "cut" is used.

In cut, all the players compete in the first three rounds. However, only the players who are usually among the top eight after the first three rounds are allowed additional three rounds to improve on their distance covered.

Player profile

A Kenyan athlete, Julius Yego, won the gold medal at the 2015 World Championship. His personal best record of 92.72 m makes him a Commonwealth as well as African Games record holder.

Wall of fame

Jan Zelezny of Czech Republic has the record of 98.48 m.

Barbora Špotáková of Czech Republic has the record of 72.28 m.

Mariya Abakumova of Russia has the record of 71.99 m.

Fact card

- A javelin may not have dimples, holes or any other modification at the tail end that would increase air drag.
- The redesigns of the javelin reduced its distance by 10%. However, these changes were carried out to prevent the javelin from falling into the audience of the stadium!
- Javelin throw is a part of the Heptathlon for women and the Decathlon for men.
- High schools in the USA hold several athletic competitions. But, javelin throw is banned in most of them as it is considered unsafe.

Shot Put

A soldier in the Siege of Troy was recorded of having picked up a stone when he ran out of arrows. He cast a boulder at the Greek army and became the first shot-putter the world knows of.

A shot put ball is made up of many materials like iron, steel, brass, sand and synthetic materials like polyvinyl.

Origin

Shot-putting occurred in ancient times with the hurling of weights and boulders, both as military training and as a display of strength. The Scottish Highlands have recorded games, which had weight tossing events as far back as the first century.

The modern sport involves the use of a round ball, made under very precise specifications. This version also has a military origin.

In the Middle Ages, the soldiers held competitions of hurling cannonballs. Shot put competitions were first recorded in Scotland, during early nineteenth century.

This game has been a part of the Olympics and requires the putter to throw a shot at the farthest distance by following a certain set of rules.

This silhouette shows the three main positions of the shot-putter while he makes a shot.

Rules

Shot put is judged on the basis of the longest legal throw, which adheres to the following rules:

- Gloves are not used but the players may tape their fingers.
- The athlete must rest the shot close to the neck and keep it tight throughout the motion.
- The shot must be released above the height of the shoulder, using only one hand.
- The shot must land in the designated sector (34.92°).

A shot-putter bracing a shot at his neck before he throws it.

The other arm s stretched out to maintain the balance and direction of the throw.

The form of the shot-putter is not only important for a good throw, but also for a good score.

The athletes may enter the ring wherever they choose to. A foul throws occur when an athlete:

- does not pause within the circle before beginning the throwing motion
- does not complete the throwing movement within 60 seconds of having his/her name called
- drops the ball below shoulder level at any point
- If the shot loses contact with the neck at any point.

The athlete must also not move outside the restricted area. Their movement is restricted as they are not allowed to touch with any part of the body (including shoes):

- the top or ends of the toe board
- the top of the iron ring
- anywhere outside the circle

The toe board that the shot-putter is not allowed to cross.

Lines drawn on the ground to measure the distance of the shot-put from the thrower.

The circle from where the shot-putter launches the shot.

Misconceptions:

There are a few urban myths associated with shot put. Some of the most common ones are noted below:

- The athlete must enter the circle from the back.
- The athlete entering the circle, then exiting and re-entering it prior to starting the throw results in a foul.
- Loose clothing, shoelaces or long hair touching outside the circle during a throw, or an athlete bringing a towel into the circle and then throwing it out prior to the put results in a foul.

None of these is an actual foul since it confers no advantage to the athlete.

Player profile

Tomasz Majewski is a shotputter who won the gold in the 2012 Olympics. He is Polish and this is his second Gold medal. He won the first one in the 2008 Olympics. He also won a silver medal in the World finals in 2009.

Wall of fame

Randy Barnes of the USA holds both outdoor and indoor men's records. He threw 23.12 m outdoors and 22.66 m indoors.

Natalia Lisovskaya of the Soviet Union holds the women's outdoor record for throwing 22.63 m in Moscow.

Helena Fibingerová is a Czech shot putter who holds the women's indoor record for throwing 22.50 m in Jablonec.

Fact card

- King Henry VII of England was an accomplished weight and hammer thrower.
- Brass and iron are usually used to make the shot, but any metal harder than brass is allowed.
- The men's shot put has been a part of the Olympics since 1896. Women's shot put was included in the Olympics in 1948.

High Jump

With a simple policy of "higher is better", high jump is one of the major athletics sport in which the players have to jump over a horizontal bar (without making it fall) kept at predefined heights.

Origin

The first modern instance of high jump was recorded in Scotland in the nineteenth century. It was probably a part of the Highland games. Since the equipment for the game is limited to a pair of shoes, the success of the players in high jump depends mostly upon their talent, skill and techniques.

Various techniques have been used in this sport. Initially, the players tried to "scissor" over the bar, which means that they put one foot over and then another. A revolutionary change in this technique was made when a player approached the bar at an angle and laid his torso parallel to his legs when scissoring. The act of lowering the torso and raising his legs gave him an additional lift to make the jump. After this, a new technique was introduced, called the "fosbury flop". Today, the most prominently used technique is called a "fosbury flop".

While attempting a high jump, the body must not touch the bar.

This sport is carried out on sports grounds, where the audience can watch from a distance.

Rules

The primary rule of the high jump is that the player must take off to jump with only one foot. The jump is considered a failure if the horizontal bar is touched or it falls.

Jumps start at a height announced by the chief judge and then the bars gets raised progressively higher and higher.

A player who misses a total of three jumps at one particular height or a combination of heights is ruled out of the competition.

If there is a tie between two players, it is resolved by:

1 Lowest number of misses at the highest height

2 Lowest number of misses in total

The western roll; a new technique introduced to do the high jump that seems to be more efficient.

Athletes wear closely fitting clothes so as not to interfere with their jump or make the bar fall.

Fact card

- In earlier games, the players would wear different shoes; one with a thicker sole on the take-off foot for a better lift and a thinner one on the other with more spikes to give more traction.